Rough Guides

25 Ultimate experiences

Middle East

Make the most of your time on Earth

ROUGH
GUIDES

25 YEARS 1982–2007

NEW YORK • LONDON • DELHI

Contents

Introduction 4-5

01 Awe-struck by the Pyramids at Giza 8-9 **02 Bedouin** camping at Wadi Rum 10-11 **03 Feasting** on Lebanese mezze 12-13 **04 Shopping** in the City of Gold 14-15 **05 Greeting** the Pharaohs in the Valley of the Kings 16-17 **06 Diving** the Gulf of Aqaba 18-19 **07 Discovering** Mada'in Saleh 20-21 **08 The moulid** of Sayyid Ahmed al-Bedawi, Tanta 22-23 **09 Floating** on the Dead Sea 24-25 **10 Experiencing** Yemen's traditional architecture 26-27 **11 Drifting** down the Nile 28-29 **12 Searching** for dragon's blood, Socotra 30-31 **13 Christmas** in Bethlehem 32-33 **14 Taking tea** in Isfahan 34-35 **15 Sand-skiing** in the dunes 16 **Walking around** the Old City of Jerusalem 36-37 **17 Relaxing** in a hammam, Damascus 38-39 **18 On the incense trail** in Arabia Felix 40-41 **19 Carving a path** through Persepolis 42-43 **20 Ramadan nights**, Cairo 44-45 **21 Sunset** over Palmyra 46-47 **22 Frolic** with dolphins off Muscat 48-49 **23 Bargaining** in the Aleppo souk 50-51 **24 Walking the Siq** to Petra 52-53 **25 Checking out** the Bauhaus architecture in Tel Aviv 54-55

Miscellany 59-72
Small print & Rough Guides info 73-79
Index 80

Introduction

EXPERIENCES have always been at the heart of the Rough Guide concept. A group of us began writing the books **25 years ago** (hence this celebratory mini series) and wanted to share the kind of travels we had been doing ourselves. It seems bizarre to recall that in the early 1980s, travel was very much a minority pursuit. Sure, there was a lot of tourism around, and that was reflected in the guidebooks in print, which traipsed around the established sights with scarcely a backward look at the local population and their life. We wanted to change all that: to put a country or a city's popular culture centre stage, to highlight the clubs where you could hear local music, drink with people you hadn't come on holiday with, watch the local football, join in with the festivals. And of course we wanted to push travel a bit further, inspire readers with the confidence and knowledge to break away from established routes, to find pleasure and excitement in remote islands, or desert routes, or mountain treks, or in street culture.

Twenty-five years on, that thinking seems pretty obvious: we all want to experience something real about a destination, and to seek out travel's **ultimate experiences**. Which is exactly where these **25 books** come in. They are not in any sense a new series of guidebooks. We're happy with the series that we already have in print. Instead, the **25s** are a collection of ideas, enthusiasms and inspirations: a selection of the very best things to see or do – and not just before you die, but now. Each selection is gold dust. That's the brief to our writers: there is no room here for the average, no space fillers. Pick any one of our selections and you will enrich your travelling life.

But first of all, take the time to browse. Grab a half dozen of these books and let the ideas percolate … and then begin making your plans.

Mark Ellingham
Founder & Series Editor, Rough Guides

Ultimate
experiences
Middle
East

The Giza Pyramids appear at first as faint shadows on the skyline behind the tacky buildings of Cairo's **Pyramids Road**; as you approach they loom magnificently out of the smog. However, up close it's hard to take them in – their shape doesn't lend itself to ground-level viewing – as you're kept rather busy jostling for position among the tour groups and trying not to get in people's snapshots. Better to fend off the relentless persistence of the horse and camel merchants, **avoid the hawkers** selling tacky souvenirs and wander over the sand to the ridge that overlooks the Pyramids from the south. There, with a bit of peace and quiet to appreciate them, you get a truly awe-inspiring view of the magnificent monuments jutting out of the desert in perfect **geometric harmony**.

The pyramid age began in the twenty-seventh century BC, when state architect Imhotep designed the Step Pyramid at

need to know

The pyramids are easily accessible from Cairo by public transport (buses and shared service taxis), or by hired cab (agree a route and price with the driver in advance). Cairo hotels can arrange this for you at a good rate; also visiting, if you wish, Zoser's Step Pyramid at Saqqara, and Snofru's Red and Bent Pyramids at Dahshur.

Saqqara as a tomb for the third-dynasty pharaoh **Zoser**. Subsequent pharaohs honed the design on pyramids at Meidum and Dahshur, tweaking the angles to make them more stable, smoothing the sides and cladding them with gleaming white limestone. The Giza trio, built around 2500 BC, mark the design's **apogee**.

Yet by the Middle Ages, the Pyramids, fallen into disrepair and their limestone cladding pilfered to make quicklime, were simply ancient ruins about which there was much speculation; the common conception was that they were treasure houses guarded by spirits. Later, nineteenth-century **European travellers** thought the pyramids were Joseph's granaries from the Old Testament; modern-day archeologists have rediscovered their true purpose and we also know that the pyramids were designed to preserve the pharaoh's *ka*, a force emanating from the sun god which brought order and stability to the whole of Egypt.

The **ancient Greeks** listed the Pyramids among the seven wonders of the world, and some four and a half thousand years later, they still live up to the title. As the locals say: "All things dread time, but time dreads the Pyramids."

2 Bedouin camping at Wadi Rum

My Bedouin guide settled forward over his *ribaba*, a simple traditional stringed instrument. As he drew the bow to and fro, the mournful, reedy music seemed to fill the cool night air, echoing back off the cliff soaring above us. The fire threw dancing shadows across the sand. A billion stars looked down.

"Bedouin" means desert-dweller. It's a cultural term: Bedouin today, whether they live in the desert or not (many are settled urban professionals), retain a strong sense of identity with their ancestral tribe. You'll find this desert culture across the Middle East, but to get a feel for its origins you need to travel into its homeland – which is why I'd come to southern Jordan, specifically Wadi Rum.

Here, the dunes and desert vistas form one of the classic landscapes of the Middle East – the backdrop for the movie *Lawrence of Arabia*. Granite and sandstone mountains rise up to 800m sheer from the desert floor. The heat during the day is intense: with no shade, temperatures down on the shimmering sand soar. Views stretch for tens of kilometres; the silence and sense of limitless space are awe-inspiring.

I'd come to spend a night camping. Camels were available as transport, but I'd opted instead for a jeep ride. Bumping out into the deep desert, we headed for camp: a distinctive Bedouin "house of hair" – a long, low tent hand-woven from dark goat's hair and pitched in the sands – would serve as quarters for the night.

As blissful evening coolness descended, the sun set over the desert in a spectacular show of light and colour, and the clarity of the unpolluted air produced a starry sky of stunning beauty.

need to know

Wadi Rum lies 300km south of Amman. Camping packages range from 1 night to weeks in the desert and include touring on foot, by camel and in 4WD jeeps. Prices start at around 20JD/US$30 per person. The best online resource is Ⓦwww.jordanjubilee.com.

3   Feasting on Lebanese
Mezze

Lebanese food is one of the great pleasures of travel in the Middle East, and the mainstay of this cuisine is *mezze*. Meaning an **array of appetizers**, *mezze* is served simultaneously on small plates and can form the extended *hors d'oeuvres* of a larger meal or, often, a full meal in itself.

The concept extends far back into history: the ancient Greeks and Persians both served small dishes of nuts and dried fruits with wine as an appetizer, a tradition which continued (with a non-alcoholic beverage) throughout the **medieval Arab period**.

Today, good restaurants might have thirty or forty choices of *mezze* on the menu, ranging from simple dishes of herbs, olives and pickled vegetables, *labneh* (tart yoghurt), and dips such as *hummus* (chickpea) and *baba ghanouj* (aubergine), up to grander creations like *kibbeh* – the national dish of Lebanon, a mixture of cracked wheat, grated onion and minced lamb pounded to a paste, shaped into oval torpedoes and deep-fried, *tabbouleh* (another Lebanese speciality: parsley and tomato salad with cracked wheat), *shanklish* (spiced goat's cheese), *warag aynab* (stuffed vine leaves) and so on. *Kibbeh nayeh* (lamb's meat pounded smooth and served raw) is perhaps the **most celebrated** of all *mezze*, while mini-mains such as lamb or chicken shish kebabs, charcoal-roasted larks and even seafood are also common. Everything is always accompanied by unlimited quantities of **hot, fresh-baked flat bread**, used for scooping and dipping.

Mezze exist to slow down the process of eating, turning a solitary refuelling into a convivial celebration of **good food and good company**. Sitting at a table swamped in colours and aromas, and eating a meal of myriad different flavours and textures, is nothing short of sensuous delight – as, indeed, it's intended to be.

need to know

Lebanese restaurants serving *mezze* can be found across the Middle East. In Lebanon itself, Beirut is the gourmet's prime destination, though the country's finest *mezze* restaurants are in the town of Zahlé.

4 Shopping in the
City of Gold

Dubai's nickname, the "**City of Gold**", is well earned: gold jewellery is sold here at some of the world's most competitive prices and shopping among the constant flow of customers, many here for their marriage dowries, is an exceptional experience.

The **Gold Souk** is a fascinating warren of tiny shops and stalls clustered together in the old quarter of Deira. Visit in the cool of early evening when the souk is at its best, with lights blazing and window-shoppers out in force. Every corner is crammed with jewellery of every style and variety; spotlights pick out choice pieces and racks holding dozens of sparkling gold bangles and chains dazzle the eye.

Buying is a cagey but always **good-natured** process: treat it as the chance to have a friendly chat with the shopkeeper, talking about family, work, life – anything but the item you've got your eye on. Then ask to see a few pieces, while surreptitiously assessing quality and sizing up your adversary, before lighting on the piece you knew you wanted from the start.

When the time comes to discuss money, bear in mind that the **gold price** fluctuates daily – and every shopkeeper in the souk knows the current price to several decimal places. Whereas in the West gold jewellery is sold at a **fixed price**, in Dubai the cost of each item has two separate components: the **weight** of the gold and the **quality of craftsmanship** involved in creating it. The former is fixed, according to the daily price-per-gramme (listed in the newspaper) set against the item's purity; the latter is where **bargaining** comes into play, with you and the shopkeeper trading prices – always with a smile – until you reach agreement.

It takes a cool head, amidst all that glittering gold, not to be dazzled into paying over the odds, but the experience is more than worth it.

need to know
Most shops in the Deira Gold Souk follow similar hours (daily, roughly 9am–10pm).

Greeting the Pharaohs in the Valley of the *Kings*

They're dim, hot and claustrophobic. They're packed with sweating, camera-toting tour groups. But nowhere else can you get so vivid a glimpse of ancient Egypt than in the 3000-year-old tombs where the ancient dynasties of Thebes laid their rulers to rest – in the Valley of the Kings.

Thebes' temples were built on the east bank of the Nile, to greet the rising sun and celebrate life. But where the sun set was a place of death. Here, the pharaohs sank tombs into the rock to hide their embalmed bodies, decorating the subterranean passageways with images of the gods they would meet after death on their journey to immortality.

Across the river from the busy town of Luxor, the Valley of the Kings is huge, hemmed between crags in an arid desertscape under the scorching sun. The light is glaring, the heat exhausting, the air dry as dust. There are dozens of tombs, so you need to choose judiciously: Tutankhamun is an obvious draw, but Tut was a minor pharaoh and his tomb is relatively small (and commands a hefty surcharge).

Instead, go for Ramses III – one of the grandest and longest tombs, running for almost 200m under the rubbly hills. As you descend narrow steps to the tomb entrance, the walls close in; pass through the dim gateway and the floor drops further: you're in a narrow, gloomy shaft, with images of scarabs, crocodiles and dog-headed gods for company. Further down into the musty depths, you come face to face with the garishly colourful wall-paintings for which these tombs are famous: the sun god Ra journeys through the twelve gates of the underworld, harpists sing to the god of the air and pictorial spells weave magic to protect the dead pharaoh in the afterlife.

need to know

Luxor is 700km south of Cairo. Ferries, motorboats and felucca sailboats cross the Nile, from where you can proceed by bus, taxi, bike or donkey for 11km to the Valley of the Kings (daily 6am–5pm; approx US$10).

6 Diving the Gulf of Aqaba

The Red Sea – a slender inlet that divides Africa from Arabia – is one of the world's premier diving destinations and leading off from the northern tip of the sea, the Gulf of Aqaba boasts some of its best and least damaged stretches of coral. The long Egyptian coastline is filled with brash, bustling and rather commercial resorts, and Israel's slender coast around Eilat can get uncomfortably crowded, but the unsung Jordanian resort of Aqaba offers a tranquility and lack of hustle that, for many, makes it top choice in these parts.

Diving from Aqaba is simple and rewarding: the reef begins directly from the shallows and shore dives are the norm; only 100m offshore you can explore coral walls and canyons, shipwrecks and ethereal undersea gardens.

The water here is nearly always warm and the reefs exquisite. Wide fields of soft corals stretch off into the startlingly clear blue water, while huge heads of stony, hard corals grow literally as big as a house. Endless species of multicoloured fish goggle back at you from all sides: butterflyfish, angelfish and parrotfish, amongst others. Swimming among the coral you can spot turtles, rays or moray eels and, if the fates are really smiling on you, you might just be lucky enough to encounter a shark.

need to know

Aqaba International Airport is served by several major carriers. Tour operators worldwide promote specialist diving packages to the Red Sea, and dive centres in Aqaba offer PADI and other international diving courses. Try ⓦwww.seastar-watersports.com, ⓦwww.rdc.jo, ⓦwww.aquamarina-group.com or ⓦwww.diveaqaba.com.

Discovering
Mada'in Saleh

Remote and isolated in the Arabian desert, Mada'in Saleh is the location of the magnificent Nabatean city known in ancient times as Hegra. With its great, rock-cut facades carved from warm golden sandstone, this city was once an important stop on the powerful Arabian tribe's incense trail.

Built in the first century AD on the fringes of Nabatean territory, Hegra lay at a junction of trade routes. Camel caravans travelling north from the incense towns of Arabia would stop here; animals would be rested, merchants would do business, taxes would be collected. With the constant traffic and trade, Hegra prospered, and the ruins here are suitably grand.

Roaming Mada'in Saleh you'll see all the styles typical of Nabatean architecture, set against breathtaking desert landscapes. Ornate, classically influenced tombs are carved into the cliffs, displaying impressively intricate workmanship; their detailing, preserved in the dry desert air, remains crisp and sharp. Standing beneath these towering funerary edifices, you'll feel the heavy, silent heat pressing down upon you and sense that Mada'in Saleh, while devoid of tourists, is full of Nabatean ghosts.

need to know

Mada'in Saleh is in Saudi Arabia, one of the world's least accessible countries. A tiny number of tourist visas are issued each year, but only to organized groups. Business visas and Muslim pilgrimage visas are granted under strict conditions and do not permit travel beyond one or two named destinations. Three- or seven-day transit visas are occasionally issued to individuals flying or travelling overland.

With notice, hotels in Al-Ula, 23km from Mada'in Saleh – notably the **Madain Saleh Hotel** (@www.mshotel.com.sa) – can organize the necessary permits to visit the site.

8 Joining the celebrations at the
Moulid of Sayyid Ahmed al-Bedawi, Tanta

Egyptians love a good *moulid*, the **annual celebration of a local holy man.** The biggest such gathering is that of Sayyid Ahmed al-Bedawi, an **eight-day extravaganza** held every October in the otherwise nondescript Nile Delta city of **Tanta**.

*Moulid*s are dominated by the Islamic mystical movement known as **Sufism** whose members aim to get closer to God by singing, dancing and chanting themselves into a **trance-like state**. Some fifty Sufi brotherhoods erect large marquee tents decked out with cloth in red and green swirling patterns; inside they set to work chanting and beating out a rhythm on drums or tambourines as devotees perform *zikrs* (ritual dances). The *moulid* attracts some **two million pilgrims** every year, and it does get pretty intense. In the tents, crowds sway rhythmically to the chants, while the streets outside are tightly thronged with crowds of happy, excited people. The climax comes on the last night, a Friday, called *layla al-kabira* (the big night), when Sayyid Ahmed's Sufi brotherhood, the Ahmediya, parade behind their sheikh with drums and red banners.

In the less frenetic tents, further away from **Sayyid Ahmed's mosque**, you can relax with a *sheesha* (water-pipe) or a nice cup of tea, while scoffing festive treats such as roasted chickpeas, a year-round Tanta speciality, or the sugared nuts (*hubb al-aziz*) which are produced especially for the occasion.

need to know

Accommodation in Tanta is sparse – most people just bunk down in tents – so book months ahead for any hope of a room. Alternatively, you can commute from Cairo – over forty trains a day run, taking anything from 1hr to 1hr 45min (fastest are the a/c "French" trains). There are also half-hourly buses and innumerable taxis from Cairo's Aboud terminal, and often also from around Ramses station. Inevitably, pickpockets take full advantage of the dense crowds at the *moulid*, so take care.

9 Floating
on the
Dead Sea

I peered past my toes at the **burning sun**, framed between craggy mountains opposite. Bobbing gently, outstretched and motionless on the surface of the sea, I felt like a **human cork**. I tried to swim, but my body rode too high in the water and I ended up splashing ineffectually; droplets on my lips tasted horribly bitter, and the water in my eyes stung like mad.

At 400m below sea level, the **Dead Sea** – hot, hazy and the **deepest blue** – is the lowest point on Earth and is named for its uniquely salty water, which kills off virtually all marine life. Normal seawater is three or four

percent salt, but Dead Sea water measures over **thirty percent**. The lake is fed mainly by the **River Jordan**, but due to geological upheavals it has no outflow; instead, the sun evaporates water off the surface at the rate of millions of litres a day, leading to salt and minerals – washed down from the hills by the river – crystallizing onto the beach in a **fringe of white**.

The high salt content makes the water so buoyant that it's literally impossible to sink. As you walk in from the beach you'll find your feet are **forced up from under you** – you couldn't touch the bottom if you tried – and the water supports you like a cradle. **Floating is effortless.**

The heat was oppressive and the air, with an unmistakeable whiff of sulphur, lay heavy in my nostrils. All sound was dampened by a **thick atmospheric haze** of evaporation and the **near silence** was eerie. As I lay, taking in the entire surreal experience, I realized just how aptly named this place is: the Dead Sea really feels dead.

need to know

There are hotels and/or public beaches on the eastern shore near Swaymeh (Jordan); and on the western shore at Ain Feshka (in the Palestinian Territories), Ein Gedi and Ein Bokek (both in Israel).

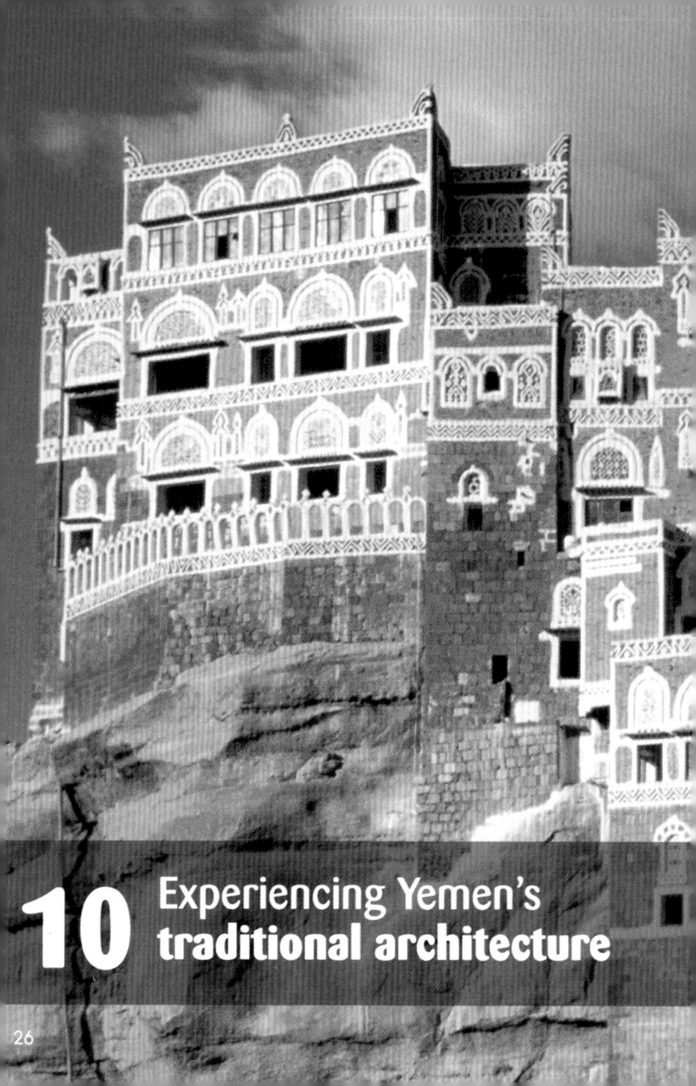

10 Experiencing Yemen's traditional architecture

Arriving in Yemen and plunging straight into the old quarter of the capital, Sanaa, is a **surreal experience**. All the bustle, familiar from Arab cities across the Middle East, is there with craft-sellers, textile merchants and all the smells – but instead of the backdrop being modern breezeblock or brutalist concrete, you're surrounded by **perfectly preserved** traditional Yemeni architecture. This ornate style, found nowhere else, is at its best in Sanaa and makes you feel as if you've been transported to **another world**.

You have to crane your neck to take in the forests of tower-houses, built on stone foundations that often date back **more than a millennium**, and rising to six or eight storeys of mud-brick. Each has details of its exterior, such as the frames of the uppermost half-moon windows, overlaid with a whitewash of lime, giving a striking, **gingerbread-house look** that is unique to Yemen. Many of the highly decorative windows are inlaid with stained glass, which shed a multicoloured glow after dark. Sanaa is spectacularly good-looking, and more than 2500 years old; you could easily spend days roaming its **labyrinthine souk**, exploring these thick-walled traditional buildings and getting under the skin of what is a **famously easygoing** capital.

East of here, in the ancient desert town of **Shibam**, still enclosed by its fortified wall, the same trademark architecture predominates. Here the concentration of tower-houses is so dense that the British explorer Freya Stark dubbed it "the **Manhattan of the Desert**". Down at dust level amidst a looming thicket of ancient, organic buildings, Shibam is not so much claustrophobic as **all-enveloping**: sandy earth tones and mud-and-lime gingerbread decoration fill the eye, from ground level virtually to the sky – a shelter from the harshness of the sun and the desert.

need to know
Shibam is roughly 500km east of Sanaa, most easily reached by air.

11 Drifting down the Nile

Egypt, often called "the gift of the Nile", has always depended on the river as a life source. Without the Nile, this country could not survive, and would not have nurtured the great civilizations of its **pharaonic** past.

Snaking the full length of the country, the Nile flows **from south to north** and boats of all varieties ply it day and night. For an authentic – and uniquely Egyptian – taste of river life, opt for a voyage on a **felucca**.

These traditional, lateen-sailed **wooden vessels** – used on the Nile since antiquity – are small: our group of six fitted comfortably. We'd negotiated in **Aswan**, Egypt's southernmost city, for a two-night trip downriver; bargaining and gathering supplies was frenetic, but as soon as the captain guided the boat out onto open water, all the bustle faded away. There was nothing to do but lie back and soak up the atmosphere.

Our stately progress and the **drowsy heat** during the day were countered by the cooler evenings, with the boat moored in the shallows and the captain cooking up a simple meal on board.

It felt timeless. Drifting gently down the **Nile** in a traditional wooden boat, shaded from the African sun by a square of colourful cloth, watching the fields and palm groves slide past, kids waving from the banks. Nothing could be more seductive.

It wasn't timeless, of course: the cloth was polyester, the kids had trinkets to sell and there were Japanese pickups parked in the shoreside villages – but **a man can dream...**

need to know

Aswan lies 900km south of Cairo. The Aswan tourist office will recommend trustworthy felucca captains, and suggests a price of approximately US$65, excluding food and (nominal) registration fees, for six people to ride from Aswan to Edfu, 105km north. The trip takes three days and two nights.

12 Searching for **dragon's blood, Socotra**

The island of Socotra – Yemeni territory, though it lies closer to Somalia than Arabia – is the most far-flung and unique destination in the Middle East. Cut off from the mainland for half the year by monsoon winds and high seas, Socotra has developed a unique ecosystem. Much of its flora is endemic to the island – odd flowers, strange plants, weirdly shaped trees. Add in the misty mountains and sense of isolation, and Socotra looks and feels like a prehistoric world.

Coming into the capital, Hadibo, you'll be struck first by the mountains – sheer pinnacles of granite soaring into the clouds behind the town. Next you'll squint sceptically at the bizarre bottle-shaped trunks of the cucumber trees in the foothills, as the feeling of entering a bizarre parallel universe heightens. But the real curiosity here, perching on the crags of the mountains, are the outlandish *Dracaena cinnabari*, or dragon's blood trees – Socotra's most famous residents.

Also called "inside-out umbrella" trees, they resemble giant mushrooms in silhouette, with a thick trunk sweeping up to a broad cap of dense foliage, sup-

ported by spoke-like branches. They look like something out of *Alice in Won-derland* – or one of Willy Wonka's absurd creations. Blink hard, but they're really there.

Socotrans still gather the reddish dragon's blood tree sap, known as cin-nabar – once used as a cure-all by the Romans. It was employed in alchemy and witchcraft in medieval times; Europeans believed that this mysterious crimson resin was the authentic dried blood of dragons and it's considered a magical ingredient in Caribbean voodoo. Hold a piece up to the sun – when it begins to glow blood-red, you'll understand why.

need to know

Socotra lies 500km south of the Yemeni coast, reached most easily by sched-uled flights from Aden or Sanaa; fares vary widely, up to around US$300 round-trip. There are plenty of hotels and guesthouses in the capital, Hadibo. For more information log on to ⊛www.socotraisland.org and ⊛www.friend-sofsoqotra.org.

13 Christmas at the Church of the Nativity in Bethlehem

Everyone has an image of Bethlehem in their minds: a quaint, humble town where Israel's messiah was born in a stable and attended by shepherds, while wise magi followed his star from the east; the reality won't disillusion you. Though battered by the strife of **occupation and intifada**, Bethlehem remains a friendly and unassuming little town. At its heart lies the Church of the Nativity, a sanctuary which might not be quite as holy as Jerusalem's Holy Sepulchre, but surely holds a fonder place in Christian hearts.

One of the oldest in the world, the church was first erected by the Roman emperor Hadrian as a **shrine to Adonis** to prevent Christian worship at the place where Jesus was born; ironically, that is how we know where it was. In 339 AD, Helena, mother of the Christian emperor Constantine, had the church put up to replace the shrine. From the outside, it looks more like a fortress, and it actually performed that function in 2002 when a mixture of militants, civilians and peace activists were kept under siege for five weeks by Israeli troops.

Queues of devotees wait patiently to pass through the hallowed precincts. Most are elderly, brought in by the coachload for the **pilgrimage of a lifetime**. Many clutch crucifixes or rosaries, some praying fervently, some weeping in awe. Inside, the church is sombre and dark: a big, cold space, broken by pillars that seem only to deepen the gloom. But the real attraction lies beneath in the Grotto of the Nativity, into which you descend by one set of stairs, coming back up by another. In the grotto, a star, like the "X" on a treasure map, marks the **exact spot where Jesus was born**, and altars mark the location of the manger and the place where the magi knelt in adoration. And if it appears rather unlike a stable to you, don't forget that in first-century BC Palestine, people usually kept their animals in caves.

For a Christian, the greatest time to visit the Church of the Nativity is of course **Christmas Eve**, when a midnight mass is held and candle-waving crowds brave the cold to gather outside in Manger Square. Here, in the magic of the moment, you can truly feel the spirit of Christmas, right where it all began.

need to know

There's little accommodation in Bethlehem, and most people make their base in Jerusalem, just 10km up the road, and joined by frequent buses and service taxis. There are, however, three places to stay in Manger Square, including a pilgrims' hospice run by the Franciscans; book well in advance.

You could easily devote a day to exploring Isfahan's great Maydan Naqsh-i Jahan, a vast rectangular space dotted with gardens, pools and fountains and ringed by arcades, above which rise the domes of the adjacent mosques. Separate from the bustle of this cultured city, it has even managed to cling onto its original polo goals, though the game hasn't been played here for centuries.

The square is always busy with people. It spreads south from the sprawling Bazar-e Bozorg, packed with shops offering Isfahan's most famous export – hand-woven Persian carpets. As you stroll the square you may well find yourself engaged in conversation by an eminently courteous Iranian with impeccable English, who turns out to have a brother/uncle/cousin with a carpet shop – where, of course, there's no charge for looking…

Even if you're able to resist the charms of the carpet bazaar, you won't be able to ignore the square's exquisite seventeenth-century Islamic architecture. To the south is the Imam Mosque, its portal and towering dome sheathed in glittering tiles of turquoise and blue, while to one side, the smaller Sheikh Lotfollah Mosque – marked by a dome of cream-coloured tiles which glow rosy pink in the afternoon sun – is, if anything, even more stunning, with fine mosaics and a dizzyingly decorated interior. Opposite, the Ali Qapu Palace – an ex-royal residence – boasts a sensational view over the square from its high terrace.

Either way, be back at one of the terrace teashops as sunset approaches. The square fills with Isfahani families strolling or picnicking on the grass and you get a grandstand view over the scene, sipping *chay* (tea) as floodlights turn the arcades, domes and minarets to gold.

need to know

Isfahan, also spelled Esfahan, is around 450km south of Tehran. The **Imam Mosque**, **Sheikh Lotfollah Mosque** and **Ali Qapu Palace** are all open daily (approx 8am–sunset; IR30,000/US$3 each).

Taking tea in

Isfahan

14

15 Sand-skiing
in the dunes

Skiing in the desert? You don't have to go to Dubai's super-cooled ski dome to experience it.

Launching yourself down the slopes under a scorching desert sun is possible in **Qatar** (pronounced something like *cutter*), a small Gulf country midway between Kuwait and Dubai – but forget about snow machines and fake icicles. Here, the ski slopes are all natural.

Jaded ski bums looking for a new thrill should take a 4WD trip to Khor al-Adaid – known as Qatar's **Inland Sea**. This is a salt-water **inlet** from the blue waters of the Gulf which penetrates far into the desert interior and is surrounded on all sides by monumental formations of giant, silvery **sand dunes**.

These are almost all crescent-shaped **barchan** dunes. Both points of the crescent face downwind; between them is a steep slip face of loose sand, while the back of the dune, facing into the breeze, is a shallow, hard slope of wind-packed grains.

This formation lends itself particularly well to **sand-skiing** or, perhaps more commonly, **sand-boarding**, both of which are identical to their more familiar snow-based cousins – except offering a **softer landing** for novices. The 4WD delivers you to the top of the dune, whereupon you set off down the loose slip face, **carving** through the soft sand to the desert floor; friction is minimal, and this kind of dry, powdery sand lets you glide like a dream.

And Khor al-Adaid comes into its own as **sunset** approaches. With low sunshine illuminating the creamy-smooth slopes and glittering light reflected up off the calm surface of the *khor*'s blue waters, a surreal, almost **mystical** quality settles on the dunes. Après-ski with a difference.

need to know

Khor al-Adaid lies 75km south of Doha, the Qatari capital. No roads run even close. The only way to get here is in a 4WD vehicle – most conveniently organized by any of several tour companies based in Doha, such as **gulf-adventures.com**. These trips, which include sand-skiing or sand-boarding on request, also take in extras such as barbecues, traditional music and overnight camping.

16 Walking around the Old City of Jerusalem

For a place so dear to so many hearts, and so violently fought over, the walled Old City of Jerusalem is not as grandiose as you might imagine; it's compact and easy to find your way around, though you'll stumble at almost every turn over holy or historic sites. The streets hum with activity: handcarts, sellers of religious artefacts, Jews scurrying through the Muslim quarter to pray at the Wailing Wall, and Palestinian youths trying to avoid the attentions of the Israeli soldiers patrolling the streets.

The three biggest attractions are the major religious sites. The Church of the Holy Sepulchre is a dark, musty, cavernous old building, reeking of incense, and home to the site of the crucifixion. Pilgrims approach the church by the Via Dolorosa, the path that Jesus took to his execution, observing each Station of the Cross and not infrequently dragging large wooden crosses through the narrow streets, where local residents pay them scant attention.

need to know

Jerusalem is easily reached from Tel Aviv's Ben Gurion airport, with regular flights from Britain, North America and Europe. There's plenty of budget accommodation in the Old City, but posher establishments are all outside the city walls. **Abu Shukri's** is at the fifth station of the cross on the Via Dolorosa, near the Damascus gate. You'll need to check the political situation when planning a visit; tensions between Israel and the Palestinians don't always affect Jerusalem itself.

Heading through the heart of the Old City, past a meat market, piled high with offal and sheep's heads, you emerge blinking into the sun-drenched esplanade that fronts Judaism's holiest site, the Western ("Wailing") Wall, last remnant of the ancient Jewish Temple that was originally built by King Solomon and later rebuilt by Herod. From here, you can nip into the Western Wall Tunnels that run under the city's Muslim Quarter; with subterranean synagogues, underground gateways and ancient aqueducts, they're fascinating to explore.

Around the side of the Wailing Wall, up on Temple Mount, is the Dome of the Rock, Islam's third-holiest site. This is the spot where Abraham offered to sacrifice his son to God, and where Mohammed later ascended to Heaven upon a winged steed. The perfect blue octagon topped with a golden dome is a fabulous gem of Ummayad architecture, immediately recognizable as the symbol of Jerusalem.

The wealth of sights in this ancient, entrancing city is overwhelming, so don't forget to make time on your wanderings for more mundane pleasures: a cardamom-scented Turkish coffee at the café just inside the Damascus Gate, or hummus at Abu Shukri's, arguably more divine than anything religious.

17

Relaxing in a **Hammam, Damascus**

Hammams – or "Turkish" steam baths – are often inconspicuous from the street, with nondescript, run-down facades. Inside though, the best of them – like the *Hammam Nur ad-Din* in Damascus – are architecturally splendid, with fountains, grand, tiled halls and coloured glass set into domed roofs to admit shafts of sunlight. Gloomy warrens of passages snake off from the entrance into the steamy distance, flanked by sweatrooms and plunge pools. The Nur ad-Din has been in operation since the twelfth century and the sense of history here is every bit as powerful as it is in the ruins and museums outside.

After depositing your clothes in a locker and donning a towel-cum-loincloth – modesty is always preserved for men, although women can strip off completely head first for a scaldingly hot sauna, your body stewing in its own juices as you lie on a marble slab working up the mother of all sweats. Public hammams are always single-sex: some admit only men, while others may publicize set hours for women (and children), when male staff are replaced by female counterparts.

An ice-cold shower follows, after which you can expect to be approached by a heavily built, no-nonsense attendant bearing a rough-textured glove, used to scrub every inch of your body and loosen layers of dirt and dead skin you didn't even know you had.

You may then be offered a massage, which often involves much pummelling and joint-cracking. With your circulation restored to maximum and every sinew tingling, seemingly endless rounds of soaping, steaming, splashing and cold plunging follow, for as long as you like, at the end of which you'll be swaddled in towels and brought a refreshing glass of sweet tea to aid recovery. Sheer heaven.

need to know

Hammam Nur ad-Din (daily 8am–midnight) is strictly men-only; a full session costs around S£250/US$5. **Hammam al-Qaimariyya** (daily 7am–midnight) is one of several in Damascus with women-only hours (noon–5pm).

18 On the
incense trail
in Arabia Felix

In antiquity, the Romans knew southern Arabia – the area of modern **Yemen** and the far southwestern tip of **Oman** – as **Arabia Felix**, meaning fortunate. This rugged land was so named for its fabulous wealth, derived from trade in **exotic goods** such as spices, perfumes, ivory and alabaster (most of which were brought from India) and, above all, locally cultivated **frankincense** and **myrrh**.

The **incense trail** was followed, in ancient times, by camel caravan from **Salalah**, regional capital of Oman's **Dhofar** region and traditionally regarded as the source of the world's finest frankincense, to Petra in Jordan.

Plunging into the alleys of Salalah's **souk** is a heady experience. Here, hemmed in by **coconut groves**, stalls and shops are crammed tightly together, offering everything from snack foods to textiles and jewellery. The air is filled with the cries of hawkers, the sweet smell of perfumes and the rich, lemony scents of frankincense and myrrh.

Prohibitively expensive commodities in the ancient world, frankincense and myrrh were offered by two of the wise men as gifts to the newborn Jesus Christ. They were also essential to religious ritual in every temple in every town. **Buying** them today is a fascinating business: shopkeepers will show you **crystals** of varying purity, sold by grade and by weight; sniff each before choosing. Coals and an ornate little pottery burner complete the purchase.

After Salalah, you can follow your own incense trail and, if spending several months on a camel to Petra doesn't appeal, try driving west towards the **Yemeni border** on a spectacular coast road that skirts undeveloped beaches before climbing into mountains lush with frankincense trees – or head for the lost city of **Ubar**, legendary centre of Arabia's frankincense trade, reputed to lie near **Shisr**, the location of Oman's most highly prized groves.

need to know
Salalah is 1000km southwest of Muscat, served by regular flights. A quarter-kilo of frankincense, with a burner, costs about US$2.80.

19 Carving a path through
Persepolis

You begin to feel the historical weight of Persepolis as you drive down the tree-lined approach, long before reaching the actual site. Here, on the dusty plain of Marvdasht at the foot of the Zagros mountains, the heat is ferocious, but nothing can detract from the sight before you: a once-magnificent city, looming high above the plain on a series of terraces.

Enter through the massive, crumbling stone Gate of All Nations, adorned with cuneiform inscriptions that laud the mighty Persian emperor whose father built the city across a gap of 2500 years, "I am Xerxes, king of kings, son of Darius…". Walking between great carved guardian bulls standing to attention on either side of the gate, you come out on a vast terrace, stretching almost 500 metres along each side.

It's not the scale though, but the details – specifically the carvings – that make Persepolis special. Wherever you look, they indicate what went on in each area: in private quarters, bas-reliefs show servants carrying platters of food; in the Hall of Audience, Darius is being borne aloft by representatives of 28 nations, their arms interlinked. Everywhere you can trace the intricately worked details of curly beards and the even more impressive expressions of body language that show the skill of the ancient artists.

The centrepiece is the ruined Apadana Palace, where you come nose-to-nose with elaborately carved depictions of the splendours of Darius the Great's empire – royal processions, horse-drawn chariots and massed ranks of armed soldiers. Look closer and you'll spot human-headed winged lions, carved alongside esoteric symbols of the deity Ahura Mazda. Begun around 518 BC by Darius to be the centrepiece of his vast empire, Persepolis was a demonstration of Persian wealth and sophistication – and it shows.

need to know

Persepolis – known locally as **Takht-e Jamshid** – lies 55km northeast of Shiraz, a cultured and stylish city. The site is open daily (March–Oct 6am–6pm, July & Aug until 8pm, Nov–Feb 8am–5pm; IR30,000).

20
Ramadan nights, Cairo

Dusk is falling and everyone is out on the street. After a day spent under the **burning sun**, with reserves of patience and blood-sugar at zero, Cairo's fasting millions all seem intent on **letting their hair down** at the same time.

You might think visiting Cairo during Ramadan is a bit perverse. This ninth month of the Muslim calendar was when Prophet Muhammad received his **first revelation** and is, consequently, holy: Muslims abstain from eating, drinking and smoking during daylight hours. But while the days are tough, with tempers on a short fuse, after dark you get to join in with what feels like a **citywide carnival**.

As sunset approaches, Cairenes move at a **blistering pace**, scampering to catch buses and weaving heedlessly through the traffic. Everyone is rushing to be in place at table when the mosques sound the **call to prayer** – the sign that the day's fasting is over. Many restaurants open for *iftar* (the sunset meal): take your place at a communal bench and then wait until the mosques sound the call. Traditionally, you break the fast with dates, and then everyone tucks into *fuul* (beans) in simple cafés or lavish buffets in the poshest eateries – always in a welcoming spirit of **shared endeavour**. Restaurants overflow with people, scoffing happily together under traditional decorative Ramadan lanterns.

As the evening rolls on, the **party spirit takes hold**. Dressed-up Cairenes pack the streets. Lights blaze. Traffic toots. Firecrackers erupt. All the souks – including the famous Khan el-Khalili bazaar – do a roaring trade. Whirling dervishes perform in the squares and live music concerts take place across the city. Full-scale partying continues into the **small hours** – whereupon *suhour*, the dawn meal, marks the start of another day's fasting.

need to know
Non-Muslims are not expected to fast. Restaurants in the big hotels serve breakfast and lunch behind closed doors.

21
Sunset over
Palmyra

Sunsets make the desert come alive. The low, rich light brings out textures and colours that are lost in the bleached-out glare of noon. It had been a hot, dusty day, but now, perched on a summit high above the desert floor, with the sun at our backs, the views made it all worthwhile.

Spread out below us was the ruined city of Palmyra. For most of the second and third centuries AD, this was one of the wealthiest and most important trading centres in the eastern Roman Empire, perfectly positioned at the fulcrum of trade between Persia and Rome.

We'd spent the day exploring its fabulously romantic array of semi-ruined temples and tombs, their honey-coloured stonework bronzed by the desert sun.

Inside the huge Temple of Bel, we'd stood where the Palmyrenes' chief deity was worshipped alongside the gods of the moon and the sun. And we'd walked the length of Palmyra's Great Colonnade, an ancient street more than a kilometre long, flanked by tall columns and set amidst the sandy ruins of temples, marketplaces, a theatre and other buildings which once formed the core of the city.

Overlooking us from the west were the ramparts of a ruined, seventeenth-century Arab castle. As sunset approached, we'd ventured up here. It was then that Palmyra's most evocative tale hit home.

At the height of the city's wealth and influence, in 267 AD, Queen Zenobia led her army against the might of Rome, rapidly seizing the whole of Syria and Egypt. Rome hit back, sacking Palmyra in 273 and parading Zenobia in chains through the streets of Rome – but those few short years of rebellion created a legend: Zenobia as the most powerful of Arab queens, Palmyra as her desert citadel.

need to know

Palmyra is 220km northeast of Damascus. The site is unfenced, though some of the temples have set hours (generally 8am–sunset; S£300/US$6). There are dozens of hotels in the adjacent town of Tadmor.

Tightly wedged along a coastal strip between the Hajar mountains and the blue waters of the Gulf, **Muscat** in Oman has been called the Arabian Peninsula's most enigmatic capital for its bewildering mixture of conservative tradition and contemporary style. Muscat itself – the walled, seafront quarter that hosts the **Sultan's Palace** – is one of three towns comprising the city. Inland lies the busy, modern area of **Ruwi**, while a short walk along the coast from Muscat is **Mutrah**, site of the **souk** and daily **fish market** – but the city's unmissable attraction is the astonishing display of marine acrobatics to be seen daily just offshore.

Dolphins are the star performers, dancing and pirouetting on the water in the sparkling sunlight. From various points along the coast near Muscat, tour operators run **dolphin-watching** trips, departing around 6.30 or 7am. The early start is worth it, as each morning numerous pods of dolphins congregate beside the little boats including common, bottlenose and the aptly named **spinner dolphins**, which delight in somersaulting out of the water with eye-popping virtuosity, directly under your gaze. Adults and youngsters alike take part, seemingly showing off to each other as well as the goggling humans; nobody knows why they spin, but they do it every morning, before sliding off into deeper waters. **Whales** have also been sighted close to shore in the winter months (Oct–May), amongst them humpbacks and even **killer whales**.

And if that's not enough, you can return at **sunset** for more dolphin-watching, or alternatively even take to the water yourself for a closer look: **kayaking** with the dolphins, morning or evening, is a real treat. Paddling a short distance into the midst of the frolicking beasts brings you close enough to interact with them, their squeaks and clicks filling the air

need to know
Omani operators offering dolphin-watching cruises include **arabianseasafaris. com**, **omandiving.com** and **zaharatours. com**. Prices are around US$65 per person for the basic trip, more for extras such as kayaking.

"Best price to you, my friend!" are familiar words to anyone who's tried to strike a deal in a Middle Eastern souk. To buy here you have to bargain – prices are always open to discussion.

Shopping in these bazaars is, for many visitors, the epitome of the Middle Eastern experience. With busy, narrow, shop-lined lanes crowded with people, souks are always redolent with the aroma of food and spices mingling with the stink of animals; they're packed with sights and sounds and full of atmosphere.

Aleppo's souk is one of the best. You can get lost here time and time again, roaming the dimly lit lanes past windows full of gold jewellery and stalls piled high with rope or soap or ice cream. Hit the wall as donkey-carts and minivans force a path through the shoppers; linger among the perfume shops, sample fresh almonds and finger exquisite silks.

If you're after a particular item, play it cool. Work out the most you would be prepared to pay – then take the time to chat. In the souk, shopkeepers are never in hurry; they want to talk, pass the time of day, offer you a glass of tea and a sit-down – whether you're a customer or not.

Eventually you can casually enquire how much the item costs. The first price quoted will be twice, perhaps three or four times, as much as the shopkeeper would be prepared to accept, so counter it with a low offer of your own. In response he'll tut, knit his brows, perhaps wag a finger at you – it's all part of the game.

There are only two rules to bargaining: never lose your temper, and never let a price pass your lips that you're not prepared to pay. And don't forget: the "best price" never is. In the souk, everyone's a sucker.

Bargaining
in the
Aleppo
souk

23

need to know

Aleppo is 350km north of Damascus and is accessible by plane, train and bus. Most shops in the souk are open 9am to 6pm (closed on Fridays).

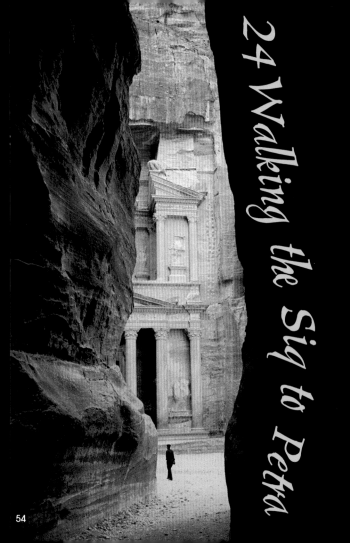

24 Walking the Siq to Petra

Tucked away between parallel rocky ranges in southern Jordan, Petra is awe-inspiring. Popular but rarely crowded, this fabled site could keep you occupied for half a day or half a year: you can roam its dusty tracks and byways for miles in every direction.

Petra was the capital of the Nabateans, a tribe originally from Arabia who traded with, and were eventually taken over by, the Romans. Grand temples and even Christian-era church mosaics survive, but Petra is known for the hundreds of ornate classical-style facades carved into its red sandstone cliffs, the grandest of which mark the tombs of the Nabatean kings.

As you approach, modern urban civilization falls away and you are enveloped by the arid desert hills; the texture and colouring of the sandstone, along with the stillness, heat and clarity of light bombard your senses. But it's the lingering, under-the-skin quality of supernatural power that seems to seep out of the rock that leaves the greatest impression.

As in antiquity, the Siq, meaning "gorge", is still the main entrance into Petra – and its most dramatic natural feature. The Siq path twists and turns between bizarrely eroded cliffs for over a kilometre, sometimes widening to form sunlit piazzas in the echoing heart of the mountain; in other places, the looming walls (150m high) close in to little more than a couple of metres apart, blocking out sound, warmth and even daylight.

When you think the gorge can't go on any longer, you enter a dark, narrow defile, opening at its end on to a strip of extraordinary classical architecture. As you step out into the sunlight, the famous facade of Petra's Treasury looms before you. Carved directly into the cliff face and standing forty metres tall, it's no wonder this edifice starred in *Indiana Jones and the Last Crusade* as the repository to the Holy Grail – the magnificent portico is nothing short of divine.

need to know

Petra (daily 6am–sunset; JD21/US$30) is 240km south of the Jordanian capital, Amman. The adjacent town of Wadi Musa has restaurants and hotels ranging from five-star to backpacker.

Checking out the
Bauhaus architecture
in Tel Aviv

Tel Aviv is a city with chutzpah, a loud, gesticulating expression of urban Jewish culture; revelling in a Mediterranean-style café culture it has dozens of bars and clubs – all aimed squarely at the under-30s. Founded in 1909, it's not likely to have much in the way of architectural interest, or so you'd think. Take a closer look and Tel Aviv reveals a wealth of buildings constructed in the International Style, inspired by the German Bauhaus school. Not as grandiose as its predecessor, Art Deco – indeed, deliberately understated in contrast – this style has its own charm, and abounds in Tel Aviv as nowhere else in the world.

Wandering the streets, you don't at first see the architecture, but then you start to notice it, and suddenly you'll see it everywhere – it really is a signature of the city. The International Style's beauty lies not in ornamentation or grand gestures, but in its no-nonsense crispness: lines are clean, with lots of right-angles; decoration is minimal, consisting only of protruding balconies and occasionally flanged edges, designed to cast sharp shadows in the harsh Mediterranean sunlight; and it wears whitewash especially well, giving the whole of Tel Aviv an almost Hockneyesque feel with its straight white lines and hard edges, as if someone had turned up the contrast button just a mite too high.

Check it out on Rehov Bialik, a small residential street in the very centre of town. Take a stroll on Sederot Rothschild, a fine 1930s avenue with some very classic Bauhaus buildings. A further wander around the streets in between Bialik and Rothschild yields still more examples of the genre, as does a visit to the more workaday district of Florentin.

Cool and stylish as its cafés, Tel Aviv's architecture reflects the attitude of the city itself – young, brash and straightforward. Like the city, it may not impress at first, but it definitely grows on you.

need to know

Tel Aviv is served by regular El Al flights from Britain, North America and Europe, as well as flights on BA and several US airlines. Even when Israel and Palestine are consumed by conflict, Tel Aviv seems a world away. Because International Style architecture looks best in strong sunlight, summer is the optimum time to see it, though be warned that the city can be stiflingly hot then.

25 Ultimate experiences

Middle East miscellany

1 Drink

The Middle East's best-known alcoholic tipple is **arak**, an aniseed spirit most famously distilled in Lebanon, which – like Israel – also has a thriving wine industry.

Shiraz once stood at the centre of a renowned wine region. Its name lives on as one of the world's most famous grapes (aka Syrah), though the city itself now lies in Iran, where the production of alcohol is effectively banned.

The Middle East's only microbrewery, producing **Taybeh** beer, is located near the Palestinian city of Ramallah.

2 People

Country or territory	Population (approx.)	Capital
Bahrain	700,000	Manama
Egypt	79,000,000	Cairo
Iran	69,000,000	Tehran
Iraq	27,000,000	Baghdad
Israel	6,400,000	Jerusalem
Jordan	6,000,000	Amman
Kuwait	2,500,000	Kuwait City
Lebanon	3,900,000	Beirut
Oman	3,200,000	Muscat
Palestinian Authority	3,500,000	–
Qatar	900,000	Doha
Saudi Arabia	27,500,000	Riyadh
Syria	19,000,000	Damascus
United Arab Emirates	2,600,000	Abu Dhabi
Yemen	22,000,000	San'a
	TOTAL: 273,200,000	

 3 Kabbalah

Kabbalah is not a religion, but a branch of **Jewish mysticism** established in the 16th century in the town of Safed (or Tzfat), in modern Israel, which uses devotional and esoteric practices to unlock the hidden meanings of the Torah (the Jewish holy book). It has become a fashion among celebrities like Madonna, who mix it with gnosticism, humanism and elements of the occult in a heady but – some say – insubstantial New Age brew.

"Squeeze the past like a sponge, smell the present like a rose and send a kiss to the future."

Arab proverb

4 Mountains

At 5671m, **Mount Damavand**, in Iran, is higher than any European peak. The summit is reachable in three days of steep walking. **Mount Sinai** (2285m), in Egypt, is venerated by Jews, Christians and Muslims as the place where God revealed the Ten Commandments to Moses. It's a popular spot from which to watch the sun rise. Near Bcharré, on the slopes of **Qornet as-Sawda**, the highest mountain in Lebanon (3090m), stands the last surviving forest of Lebanese cedar trees.

5 Literature

Naguib Mahfouz is the only writer in Arabic to win the Nobel Prize for Literature, in 1988. His most famous works, including *Midaq Alley* (1947) and *Children of Gebelawi* (1959), evoke Cairo's street life amidst a cast of colourful characters.

S.Y. Agnon is the only writer in Hebrew to win the Nobel Prize for Literature, in 1966. *The Bridal Canopy* (1931) and *Only Yesterday* (1945), two of Agnon's best-known books, use a surreal style to explore conflicts between Jewish tradition and modernity.

Simin Daneshvar's *Suvashun* (1969) explores themes of modernity in her home town of Shiraz, and is the highest-selling novel ever written in Persian.

6 Cities

The title of the world's oldest continuously occupied city is disputed by several Middle Eastern contenders, including **Damascus** in Syria, the Palestinian city of **Jericho** and **Jbeil** (Byblos) in Lebanon.

Cairo, with a population around 15 million, is the largest city in the Arab world.

7 A True Diva

The Egyptian diva **Umm Kalthoum** (also spelled in a number of other ways, including Oum Kalsoum and Om Kolsum; 1904–75) remains the best loved singer in the Arab world, outselling many contemporary stars. At her peak – the 1950s to 1970s – she was able to empty the streets of Cairo and other Arab cities, as people stopped everything to listen to her monthly radio concerts. These were nothing short of epic, often consisting of a four- or five-hour performance of a single song – generally on the themes of love, loss and yearning – to an orchestral accompaniment. An estimated **four million mourners** attended her funeral.

"If God lived on earth, people would break his windows."

Jewish proverb

8 Five great restaurants

Arabi, Zahlé, Lebanon Lining the Bardouni river in the mountain town of Zahlé are dozens of terrace restaurants serving superb Lebanese *mezze*. *Arabi* is the top choice, a great place to relax over an all-day lunch.

Fishawi's, Cairo, Egypt Set on a bustling lane in the Khan el-Khalili bazaar, this place is the epitome of the traditional Cairo coffee-house. It has been managed by the same family since 1773 and has remained perpetually open in all that time. Battered furniture, ancient gilt-edged mirrors and haughty waiters set the tone; savour the atmosphere over a pot of mint tea and a *sheesha* (hubbly-bubbly pipe).

Khayyam, Tehran, Iran One of Tehran's best-known restaurants, set in a 300-year-old building that was once part of a mosque and is now beautifully restored. The menu of classic Persian dishes is unsurpassed, and there's the added attraction of traditional music, played live nightly.

Sissi House, Aleppo, Syria A charming restaurant occupying a splendid seventeenth-century townhouse on a quiet alley in the Armenian quarter of Aleppo. The ambience is sophisticated, with candlelit tables filling an open courtyard, and the food is nothing short of exquisite.

Tannoureen, Amman, Jordan For the discerning Middle Eastern gourmet, Amman stands second only to Beirut in terms of quality of food and standards of service – and *Tannoureen* is its finest Lebanese restaurant, with sensational cuisine served in a cultured, atmospheric setting.

9 Etiquette

In all Arab cultures, knowingly showing the **soles of your feet** or shoes to someone is a direct insult. This often requires taking extra care while sitting: crossing your legs ankle-on-knee leaves a sole exposed to the person beside you; sitting on the floor requires some foot-tucking to ensure no one is in your line of fire; and putting your feet up on chairs or tables is not done.

10 "Southwest Asia"

The term "**Middle East**" asks more questions than it answers. For this book, we've included Egypt (even though Egypt is in Africa) and excluded Turkey (even though Turkey lies largely outside Europe). Other definitions reverse this choice. Until 1918, the term "Middle East" described the area from Mesopotamia (Iraq) to India. Turkey and the eastern Mediterranean were instead termed the "**Near East**" – a term now fallen into disuse. However, both these terms are Eurocentric: from an Indian or Chinese perspective, it makes more sense to say "Middle West". For this reason, the UN and other international bodies generally define the Middle East as "**West (or Southwest) Asia**".

11 Five great hotels

American Colony Hotel, Jerusalem This is the holy city's most famous hotel, more than 120 years old – genteel, sophisticated and tasteful, set in tranquil grounds.

Baron Hotel, Aleppo, Syria Once the luxurious choice of Agatha Christie and Lawrence of Arabia, the *Baron* has fallen on hard times: it's got bags of character, if you can overlook deficiencies in the ancient plumbing and bedsprings.

Burj al-Arab, Dubai, UAE Perhaps the most famous luxury hotel in the Middle East, an iconic 321m tower in the shape of a billowing sail that dominates the Dubai waterfront.

Dead Sea Mövenpick, Jordan An innovative, superbly designed five-star hotel and spa resort, looking west over the Dead Sea.

Old Cataract Hotel, Aswan This splendid Edwardian-Moorish relic on the banks of the Nile dates from 1902 and has been tastefully renovated to luxurious standards.

"Don't sleep in silk sheets until you've walked across the desert."

Persian proverb

12 The Nile

The **Nile** is the longest river in the world, at almost 6700km. It has various sources as the White Nile (above Lake Victoria) and the Blue Nile (in Ethiopia), which meet at Khartoum and flow northwards to the Mediterranean Sea.

Crocodiles, worshipped as gods by the ancient Egyptians, are common along the Nile.

The Nile Delta is one of the world's **largest**, encompassing 240km of coastline between Alexandria and Port Said.

13 Railways

The train service running today between Damascus and Amman is a remnant of the **Hejaz Railway**, built by the last Ottoman sultan in 1908 from Damascus to the holy city of Medina, in the Hejaz region of Arabia.

The scenic stretch of line from Tel Aviv to Jerusalem, which was built by the British (as the Jaffa–Jerusalem railway) in 1892, also still has a regular scheduled service. The line was recently upgraded.

Currently, the only railway on the Arabian Peninsula runs from Dammam to Riyadh, though plans are afoot to extend the line to Jeddah, thus connecting the **Red Sea** and the **Gulf**.

14 Wildlife preservation

The Arabian **oryx** is a beautiful, long-horned white antelope that is indigenous to the Middle East. Throughout the twentieth century hunting drastically reduced its numbers, until the last wild oryx was shot in Oman in 1972. **Captive breeding** programmes in the USA, Jordan, Qatar and Oman ensured the survival of the species and oryx have now been reintroduced to the wild in Israel, Jordan, Oman and Saudi Arabia, all of which – along with Qatar and the UAE – maintain herds in wildlife reserves.

15 Derivations

The primary language in the Middle East is Arabic, from which many English words are derived.

- **admiral** from *ami:r-al/ -bahr* 'ruler of the seas'
- **checkmate** from *sha:h ma:t* 'the king is dead'
- **mattress** from *matrah* 'place where something is thrown'
- **zero** from *s,ifr* 'empty'

16 Five enchanting oases

▸▸ Egypt

A circuit of oases in the Western Desert includes a night in the **White Desert** near Farafra, followed by an epic journey to **Siwa Oasis**, on the Libyan border.

▸▸ Israel

South of Beersheva in the Negev desert is the extraordinary **Ein Avdat** – a spring and waterfall of cold water, concealed in a lush canyon.

▸▸ Jordan

The string of "desert castles" (actually, Islamic-era lodges) east of Amman leads to **Azraq Oasis**, desert hideout of Lawrence of Arabia.

▸▸ Saudia Arabia

In the desert south of Dhahran lies Hofuf, a town located within the vast date-palm oasis of **Al-Hasa**.

▸▸ UAE

The romantic oasis of **Liwa**, south of Abu Dhabi, is set amidst the dunes on the edge of the famous Empty Quarter of Saudi Arabia.

"A book is a garden that you carry in your pocket."

Saadi, thirteenth-century Persian Sufi poet

17 Calendars

Where Western or Christian cultures use "BC" (Before Christ) and "AD" (Anno Domini; the Year of Our Lord), the accepted terms in Jewish and Islamic contexts are "BCE" (Before the Common Era) and "CE" (Common Era).

Many different calendars are used in the Middle East. The most important are:

Calendar	Dated from...	Type	2007 equates to...
Islamic	Muhammad's emigration to Medina	Lunar	1427–1428 AH
Jewish	The Creation	Lunisolar	5767–5768 AM
Persian	Muhammad's emigration to Medina	Solar	1385–1386 AP
Western (Gregorian)	Birth of Jesus	Solar	2007 AD/2007 CE

18 Hubbly bubbly

Water-pipes are common across the Middle East, known variously as a *nargila*, *argila*, *sheesha*, *qalyan* or **"hubbly bubbly"**. They stand on the floor, reaching to table-top height. As you suck on the mouthpiece, smoke is drawn down into the water chamber with a distinctive bubbling sound. It is cool and tastes silky smooth – utterly unlike cigarette smoke.

Contrary to myth, all the **sweet smells** drifting around Arab cafés are flavoured tobacco (honey and apple are popular): cannabis is never smoked in public.

19 Five holy cities

City	Holy in...	Because...
Haifa	Baha'i	Haifa, in Israel, is the world centre of the Baha'i faith, bedecked with shrines and gardens.
Jerusalem	Judaism	Jerusalem is the holiest city for Jews; it was the site of the Jewish Temples (destroyed in antiquity – though the Western Wall survives) and is mentioned by Jews in prayers three times daily.
Jerusalem	Christianity	Key episodes in Jesus's life took place in Jerusalem, including the Last Supper. The Church of the Holy Sepulchre – Christianity's holiest shrine – is believed to have been built where Jesus was crucified.
Jerusalem	Islam	Muslims consider Jerusalem the third holiest city, after Mecca and Medina. The Qur'an records a "night journey" of the Prophet Muhammad to "the farthest mosque" (*al-masjid al-aqsa*) – widely identified as Jerusalem.
Mecca	Islam	Mecca, in Saudi Arabia, is the holiest city in Islam, and the focus of the annual *hajj* pilgrimage. It holds the vast Sacred Mosque, within which stands the Kaaba, a small cubical building which Muslims believe was built by Ibrahim (Abraham). Muslims pray five times a day in the direction of the Kaaba.
Najaf	Islam (Shia)	Najaf, in Iraq, is the site of the tomb of Imam Ali, considered by Shia Muslims to be the founder of their religion. It is a principal centre of Shia pilgrimage and learning.
Nazareth	Christianity	Nazareth, in Israel, was where Jesus grew up and preached. Its Basilica of the Annunciation is said to be the largest church in the Middle East.

 20 Inventions

The **Sumerians**, an ancient people from southeastern Iraq, developed a network of city-states well before 3000 BC – the world's first civilization. Sumerian inventions include the **wheel**, **writing** and **agriculture**. The Sumerian clock, based on a sexagesimal system (60 seconds, 60 minutes, 12 hours), is still in use today.

Around the fifth century BC, mathematicians at Babylon, in Iraq, invented **zero**.

Byblos (or Jbeil, in Lebanon) was the source of the world's first **alphabet**, developed around 1200 BC.

> *"Let your happiness grow by giving it to others."*
>
> **Kahlil Gibran, 20th-century Lebanese poet**

21 Coffee

Coffee originated in Ethiopia but was first cultivated as a crop in **Yemen** a thousand years ago, from where it spread to Mecca, then Cairo, Constantinople and into Europe. The chocolatey-coffee flavour of **mocha** originated in a natural variety of arabica beans grown near the Yemeni port of Al-Mokha.

22 The Caliphs of Islam

For centuries following the death of the Prophet Muhammad, the head of the worldwide community of Islam was termed a caliph. Unity was rare: a group of Muslims soon disputed the succession and split away, becoming the Shia branch of Islam (standing in opposition to more mainstream Sunni Islam), and dynasties in various parts of the Muslim world often set up their own short-lived caliphates to rival the central authority. The caliphate was abolished by the secular Turkish parliament in 1924.

 23 Festivals

Lebanon's **Baalbek Festival**, held amid vast Roman temples, features world-class performers in classical music, opera and jazz, while the **Beiteddine Festival**, staged at a magnificent eighteenth-century mountain palace, concentrates on Arab music and performers. Both are held in July and August.

Jordan's **Jerash Festival**, which presents both Western and Arab music alongside dance and drama in an equally impressive Roman setting, also takes place in July.

24 Five films to watch

Divine Intervention (Palestine, 2002). Stories of Palestinian life, set against the backdrop of the occupation.

Lawrence of Arabia (UK, 1962). Epic tale of the British maverick who led the Arabs to victory in 1918.

Taste of Cherry (Iran, 1997). A touching, low-key story of a man in a midlife crisis.

Ushpizin (Israel, 2004). An Orthodox Jewish couple experience joy and despair as their prayers appear to be answered.

West Beirut (Lebanon, 1998). Two kids grow up quickly amidst the outbreak of civil war.

25 A biblical view

Mount Nebo lies in modern Jordan. From the summit, a spectacular panoramic view encompasses the Dead Sea, the Judean hills, Jericho on the banks of the River Jordan – as the Bible says, the "Land of Milk and Honey".

"And the Lord spoke unto Moses, saying 'Get thee up to Mount Nebo.' ... And Moses went up from the plains of Moab to the mountain of Nebo, and the Lord showed him all the land."
Deuteronomy 32–34

Ultimate experiences
Middle East
small print

The Middle East
The complete experience

ROUGH GUIDES – don't just travel

We hope you've been inspired by the experiences in this book. To us, they sum up what makes the Middle East such an extraordinary and stimulating region in which to travel. There are 24 other books in the 25 Ultimate experiences series, each conceived to whet your appetite for travel and for everything the world has to offer. As well as covering the globe, the 25s series also includes books on **Journeys, World Food, Adventure Travel, Places to Stay, Ethical Travel, Wildlife Adventures** and **Wonders of the World**.

When you start planning your trip, Rough Guides' new-look guides, maps and phrasebooks are the ultimate companions. For 25 years we've been refining what makes a good guidebook and we now include more colour photos and more information – on average 50% more pages – than any of our competitors. Just look for the sky-blue spines.

Rough Guides don't just travel – we also believe in getting the most out of life without a passport. Since the publication of the bestselling Rough Guides to **The Internet** and **World Music**, we've brought out a wide range of lively and authoritative guides on everything from **Climate Change** to **Hip-Hop**, from **MySpace** to **Film Noir** and from **The Brain** to **The Rolling Stones**.

Publishing information

Rough Guide 25 Ultimate experiences Middle East Published May 2007 by Rough Guides Ltd, 80 Strand, London WC2R 0RL
345 Hudson St, 4th Floor, New York, NY 10014, USA
14 Local Shopping Centre, Panchsheel Park, New Delhi 110017, India
Distributed by the Penguin Group
Penguin Books Ltd,
80 Strand, London WC2R 0RL
Penguin Group (USA)
375 Hudson Street, NY 10014, USA
Penguin Group (Australia)
250 Camberwell Road, Camberwell, Victoria 3124, Australia
Penguin Books Canada Ltd,
10 Alcorn Avenue, Toronto, Ontario, Canada M4V 1E4
Penguin Group (NZ)
67 Apollo Drive, Mairangi Bay, Auckland
1310, New Zealand
Printed in China
© Rough Guides 2007

80pp
A catalogue record for this book is available from the British Library
ISBN 978-1-84353-824-0

The publishers and authors have done their best to ensure the accuracy and currency of all the information in **Rough Guide 25 Ultimate experiences Middle East**, however, they can accept no responsibility for any loss, injury, or inconvenience sustained by any traveller as a result of information or advice contained in the guide.

1 3 5 7 9 8 6 4 2

Rough Guide credits

Editor: Sarah Eno
Design & picture research: Dan May, Coralie Bickford-Smith
Cartography: Maxine Repath, Katie Lloyd-Jones

Cover design: Diana Jarvis, Chloë Roberts
Production: Aimee Hampson, Katherine Owers
Proofreader: Kate Berens

The authors

Daniel Jacobs (Experiences 1, 8, 13, 16, 25) has contributed to numerous Rough Guides including West Africa, Egypt, India and Mexico, as well as authoring the *Rough Guide to Israel and the Palestinian Territories* and the *Rough Guide to Jerusalem* among others.

Matthew Teller (Experiences 2, 3, 4, 5, 6, 7, 9, 10, 11, 12, 14, 15, 17, 18, 19, 20, 21, 22, 23, 24, Miscellany) is the author of the *Rough Guide to Jordan* and the *Rough Guide to Switzerland* and is co-author of the *Rough Guide to the Italian Lakes*. He has spent many years working and travelling in the Middle East.

Picture credits

Cover Silhouette of person on camel, Petra, Jordan © Mitchell Funk/Getty Images

2 Jackal-headed god Anubis, painted limestone decoration in the tomb (KV57) of Horemheb, 18th Dynasty © Dagli Orti/The Art Archive

6 Syrian Aleppo souk: Middle East market © URF/f1 online/Alamy

8-9 Awe-struck by the Pyramids at Giza © Peter Wilson/DK

10-11 Bedouin storytelling After Dinner © Jeffrey L. Rotman/Corbis

12 Red pepper hummus © Sally Ullman/ Jupiter

12 Lunchtime reunion © Char Abumansoor/Alamy

14-15 Gold Souk, Dubai, United Arab Emirates © Joe Malone/Jon Arnold Images/Alamy

17 Jackal-headed god Anubis, painted limestone decoration in the tomb (KV57) of Horemheb, 18th Dynasty © Dagli Orti/ The Art Archive

18 Diving the Gulf of Aqaba © Peter Pinnock/ImageState/Alamy

20-21 Qasr al-Farid, the largest Nabatean Tomb in Mada'in Saleh © James Sparshatt/Corbis

23 The Al Tannoura Egyptian Heritage Dance Troupe performing traditional Sufi dance in Cairo, Egypt (also known as the Whirling Dervish) © Paul Gapper/Alamy

24-25 Tourist reading a magazine in the Dead Sea © Wolfgang Kaehler/Corbis

26-27 San'a' Governorate, Yemen © Viviane Moos/Corbis

28 Felucca on the Nile, Luxor, Egypt © Derek P Redfearn/The Image Bank/Getty

30-31 Grove of dragon's blood trees © Chris Hellier/Corbis

33 A Palestinian Christian worshipper lights votive candles © David Silverman/ Getty

34 Iranian Tea Service © Dave Bartruff/ Corbis

35 Families relax inside a Chai Khana (tea house) near the Imam Khomeini Square in Isfahan © Matthieu Paley/ Corbis

37 Woman sand-boarding down Dune © Nevada Wier/Corbis

38-39 Jerusalem, cityscape with Dome of the Rock © Sylvain Grandadam/Getty

40-41 Turkish baths, Damascus, Syria © John Frumm/Alamy/Hemispheres Images

43 Omani man makes incisions into a Boswellia sacra tree in the Wadi Adawnab © Mike Nelson/epa/Corbis

44-45 Palace G and sculptured stairway fragments at Persepolis © Aliki Sapountzi/ aliki image library/Alamy

47 A man performs a traditional Egyptian dance © Ron Watts/Corbis

48-49 Sunset behind the tetrapylon archeological ruins at Palmyra Syria © Bill Lyons/Alamy

50-51 Spinner Dolphin breaching © Stuart Westmorland/Corbis

52 Syrian Aleppo souk: Middle East market © URF/f1 online/Alamy

53 Market souk, area Aleppo, Haleb, Syria © Christian Kober/Alamy

54 Walking the Siq to Petra © eran yardeni/Alamy

56 Asia House, Tel Aviv, Israel © Eitan Simanor/Alamy

58 Palace G and sculptured stairway fragments at Persepolis © Aliki Sapountzi/ aliki image library/Alamy

72 Awe-struck by the Pyramids at Giza © Peter Wilson/DK

Over 70 reference books and hundreds of travel
guides, maps & phrasebooks that cover the world

Australia

Cuba

Britain

Singapore

Vietnam

New York City

BROADEN YOUR HORIZONS
www.roughguides.com

Index

a

alcohol 60
Aleppo 52
arak 60
architecture 26, 56

b

Bauhaus 56
bedouins 10
Bethlehem.................. 32
boats 28, 50

c

Cairo 8, 46
calendar 67
camping 10
Christianity 32, 38
christmas 32
churches 32, 38
cities ..14, 34, 38, 45, 46,
52, 57, 62
coffee 39, 69

d

Dead Sea 24
desert ...10, 16, 21, 27, 36,
48
diving 19
dolphins 50
dragon's blood
trees 30
Dubai 14

e

Egypt 8, 16, 22, 28, 46
etiquette 63

f

festivals 22, 32, 46, 70
film 71
food 13, 39, 46, 52

g

gold 14
Gulf of Aqaba 19

h

hammam 40
hotels 64

i

incense 42
inventions 69
Iran 34, 44
Isfahan 34
Islam 38, 46, 69
Israel 25, 32, 56

j

Jerusalem 38
Jesus 32
Jordan ..16, 20, 39, 44, 48,
54
Judaism 38, 57

l

language 65
Lebanon 13
literature 61
Luxor 16

m

Mada'in Saleh 20
mezze 13
mosques 22, 34
moulid 22
mountains... 10, 30, 61, 70
Muscat 50
music 10, 22, 62

n

Nabateans 21, 55
Nile, the 16, 28, 64
nomenclature 63

o

oases 66
Oman 42, 50

p

Palestine 32, 38
Palmyra 48
perfume 42
Persepolis 44

P

Petra 54
Pharaohs 10, 16
population 60
Pyramids 8

q

Qatar 36

r

railways 65
Ramadan 46
Red Sea 19
religion..32, 38, 46, 57, 61,
69
restaurants 13, 46, 62
rivers 16, 28, 64

s

sand-skiing 36
Saudi Arabia 21
shopping 14, 34, 42, 52
Socotra 30
souks 14, 42, 52
Sufism 22
swimming 24
Syria................40, 48, 52

t

Tanta 22
tea 34
Tel Aviv 57
temples 54

v

Valley of the Kings 16

w

water-pipes 22, 67
watersports 19, 50
Western ("wailing")
wall 39
wildlife 65
wine 60

y

Yemen 26, 30, 42